Welcome to

IRISH MOVIES

Word Scramble

In this book we have taken films which were set in or filmed in (even partially) Ireland and scrambled the letters. To make it a little easier we have scrambled each word individually.

There are 32 puzzles with containing the titles of 645 movies. Some are very well known and others a lot more obscure.

We have checked and doubled checked and all the movies listed do Have some connection with Ireland.

This book was compiled in Ireland especially for you. If you like Irish Word Puzzle books be sure to check all our books on Amazon.

Enjoy

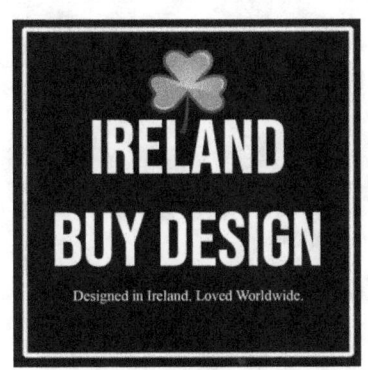

IRELAND
BUY DESIGN

Designed in Ireland. Loved Worldwide.

Irish Movies 1

AD	
3H	
HTE TIHMGY ELCT	
HTE GID	
EHT TPIIRS FO TS OILSU	
RUPE MLEU	
HTE TOLENSG CEDDAE	
TRAA AROD	
AKENT ODWN	
AMYFIL	
HONGTNI SPLROAEN	
TLLASE SYDA	
EHT DRUCE	
ERPNLUHECA ISNRGOI	
HET SEOFX FO WORAHR	
ON NEOTS EUUNRDTN	
ANUBLAEREBK	
SLNDIA FO ERTROR	
EHT ATNRMFINO	
ORGRE TSEMCANE	

NHASD	
EH	
RTYIHSO FO IMNEAC	
OHCOLS ILFE	
TOLAF KILE A FBTEURLTY	
HET IACCR	
NEISSIONRMIT	
TRREUN OT SNALCUELNAG	
RTHEE ISWE EOWNM	
STATNEA	
NSÍOI	
SYTUD IELRDAN	
ÍOINPT	
ADM TOBUA BOMAM	
EREHT HESWIS ROF MAIEJ	
HET ENIDQNETUL AOSSNE	
HTE NEHPWE	
EHT SBOY FO TS LOSUMBC	
ECNO	
RHTNAOE HORES	

HET YMEGOOBAN	
OHADSW CNRAED	
EHT DASHOW FO A NAUNMG	
ETH IRCOUER	
A PRRAEY RFO ETH GDIYN	
I NTWE NWOD	
IITACNT OTNW	
HET UKCL FO EHT IHIRS	
EHT WNDA	
CAKBL 74	
ELEGRNI NI EHT EASYR	
ILGR HIWT REEGN EESY	
NTNAEALTA	
EHT LASD	
KAEERU RTTSEE	
RACTRAH	
HROTB FO A YOB	
LFSOO FO ROEUFNT	
EON HNREUDD NNRIGSOM	
NILBD OSIVIN	

Irish Movies 4

TIOTAPRS	
IGARPMGELI	
WGGOINR PU GYA	
GNKSI	
HTE DGVABASNO	
LOULTAF	
EUTONORSIVL	
ISIKSGN CAIEDNC	
FIKCL	
TSIH SI TEH ASE	
AHAOCETSI	
ESY I CNA	
AND NDA ESBC	
GNAEELR OJHN NRGAE	
RMENDOAO	
NGHRYU ILLH	
EHT IIGSNR FO HTE OMNO	
GKINS NI RASSG LATESCS	
CIHEALM SIDEIN	
RLIECC FO NEISDRF	

A STACSMIHR RAST	
ZANOD	
PKTSACIR ADY	
NO HTE ONES	
APSYRLE FO HTE HIAFLTFU	
RNYEOO	
LERTTSCA	
A TATSE RPTAA	
HET LAWL	
YM NSHAD ERA CAYL	
TEH HRSII ONNYHEMOO	
RTA	
HOEM ULRE	
EHT YARTET	
FNNIDIG JYO	
MHNSAGNA OUHSE	
AWR FO HTE TOUNBTS	
TGAHUC NI A EREF TATSE	
ETH EPIR	
GAGRAE	

ARLDCE FO GIEUSN	
ATINACP LTFHIOOTG	
HET PKECMEAAER	
HTE ECESRT CTSIUERPR	
LEIEL	
ROMF ETH DRKA	
BEUTRLO IWHT EXS	
HET RIISH NI AIEAMRC	
EADCN LIXEE CEDAN	
GNAUEOSDR ILASISON	
HTE UARQE OLWLEF	
OMNLIHEPA	
HTE OLAHWL	
CYR FO HET NIETCONN	
LLIETT LNEIEL LELYK	
YM HSREORBT RAW	
IWAAEYSDH	
SHI OMHTRE	
NOPE PTOR	
OMCONAEDN	

ESEVN GASE	
ERDKPA	
PCANIAST NAD NGKSI	
NA ANERRG	
HET IELPCES	
BLMA	
EHT HTROALCN RAYSE	
LYBNMAUL ABYLLLU	
AFR DNA AYAW	
HTSI EOTRH EEDN	
NSUG NI HET RAEHEHT	
TEH LSPBAYOY	
ASTSET FO RFEA	
AYCTUASRN	
MRERDU NI DEEN	
AITROL	
NA ONAARSNBTN	
ILLY FO NERLKIYAL	
OCDSI SGIP	
YSHOUGBOD NI DREILAN	

ORYBLNOK	
ATRTAATC	
NEWH EHT KYS ASLFL	
ANEN EDVLIN	
ON ITERSGN ECLPA	
EOSNINAST	
HET UETQI MNA	
NI HTE YDAS FO TS TPCKIRA	
HELTNAEK NEVROUAEMN	
HET UCKL FO TEH SIRHI	
EWHN ICRLHAE EMT TTYKI	
YM LEFI ROF AENRLID	
SWIWOD EKAP	
ERECST OLEPEP	
ALHO EEFCTF	
OSER FO RALTEE	
TREPTY OLPLY	
ETH RMACH EARH	
KKCOWAGNON	
TEH SIIRH NI ICAEMAR	

EHSNENSY	
HNELE	
TEH KMAOMRBBE	
I MARDET I WKEO PU	
HET LMAROOLB FO AMCNEOR	
ILTGH YARSE WAYA	
LYON MHAUN	
HET LTAS CONURIN	
TEH GRTAE FIENAM	
AKEFIRN SIAGLTRHT	
ONFCLIONAESS	
CLNKUEK	
TEH OECLELN NBAW	
GUEAHRDT FO DASNEKRS	
,UOY EM DNA LREAMY	
BUIDNL OOODCLHLS	
OWGODTSOH	
VILAE NDA INKICKG	
HET NOTNNECI IEL	
NI ENNSSHUI RO NI DSAHWO	

A TOSL OSN	
SONMIIS OT PYRE	
NTIO EHT WTES	
TEH UQNEE FO ERNIADL	
EFRREE NDA ETH MELDO	
ITNRWES DNE	
I WSA HYPAP EHRE	
EHT TAANGREUE	
FERFALEL	
REFIGON XEGCENHA	
ERLIDAN A ATNNOI	
EIALLLG NNYEEOIDLMGN	
MENIAF OT EDROMEF	
EHT EOCELNL NABW	
ILWD ABTUO RHAYR	
A HTRGIB DBNAR WNE YDA	
HET OLNELAIMD	
EDRRIS OT HTE SAE	
ESE YUO TA ETH APLILR	
RCEPAEIEF	

HUISMLOST	
ULSRET UNRDETEHA	
IICEVSV	
EHWSLORWBLIET	
HYIWREA	
LASNI	
AEDD NLGAO HTE YAW	
TFALA TOIVDAENI	
A IGLR OFRM HUMAOGSDI	
YM RIFNDE JEO	
TEH RNFOEIMR	
OLITE DAN EM	
AKT ADN :IEALF TAERWRDE	
ETH NOILLE	
HET NGAIGHN ELGA	
ELID,RAN TEH PSPRSEDEO	
OOCKPNU	
LDERO TANH ERLINDA	
LNPIEA PNACRUELHSE	
ETH AHYDR UCBSK VEOIM	

MNAOE	
,HO RM TORRPE	
RIHSI IEDSNTY	
LYNO HET DWNI	
HTE SETCR	
LDWI SEMRCBEED	
LORL PU YRUO ELSVSEE	
AOMNDR ESSPAAG	
CETACELAPB RSIK	
SENTHTRG NDA RNOOHU	
TGILHF FO HET EODSV	
KWEA OOWD	
SSNERNI	
IRAE,HLNGS OG DNWO	
DAB ADY RFO ETH UTC	
TEH XOF FO EGARNVOLN	
SNAEG BNREWO	
HTE OBY MORF RCURYEM	
NONAT	
NCTNATENHEM	

ORYODHT MLISL	
HNEW EADNBNR TEM TRDUY	
EGIMSA	
QECNLUEAIJ	
ATC FO BELRAYTA	
TEH LPUREP XAIT	
A TTILEL BTI VT	
PESDE GNATID	
PDCTOEIEN	
AAMD NDA UPAL	
DELNHCRI TA OKWR	
EMOR HATN A IIRSCACEF	
NA RICSSI	
AETLTB FO HET BGSIDOE	
SMUASH	
STOOH OT LLKI	
TEH LNTOVIE NYMEE	
IHGH TRISSIP	
HTE DARO OT EOHERNW	
MBARE	

LSGNICO HTE IRNG	
NAM BTAUO ODG	
RYRHAS MAGE	
RLAWTTASE	
TISACOHCL	
ERSTCE FO ETH AEVC	
STPEE TMEOER	
HTE OTRNF IENL	
RKNBOE OSGN	
TEH MRKETAHCAM	
ECSRAM FO TEH EHBENSA	
FI YLNHC DHA NIVDDAE	
CLSINEE	
DRE ORSSE DNA ERPTLO	
EHSOGTA	
HTE OYNGU FERSEDONF	
TEH ERACOL	
TEH LEVDSI DRYOOWA	
HWO UTBOA OYU	
ATCIPAN TOOTBYC	

TLOS VSELI	
TEH STLA PTSBEREEM	
XPEII	
AFAEBTSKR NO LUOPT	
IHSIR RFO CKUL	
OLVSUREES LEAON	
SSOEPROFR MTI	
LLGNSAADS	
TREEBI	
SIKN NI EHT EAMG	
IISRH AMJ	
UY GMIN SI NIMA OMD	
CAVRYLA	
EHT ASLT EUAPLENCRH	
LNPLARE	
ACL	
NEWH LIA CAEM OT EDLNRIA	
HET BAKLC ESEPH	
LNEDEG FO HTE GBO	
ETH ESA	

TEH KYE	
EAHRAWD ERX	
NGSO FO HET ESA	
EMBRECDE IDBER	
SSUMCOT	
HDNOSEMA IVDEL	
EGSARHR	
RNU ADN UMJP	
NA ENDPENEDTNI OPEPLE	
RRAETUSE SLIDNA	
OZO	
ELARTRACOEC	
A AEDT RFO MDA RAMY	
MIMJSY LLAH	
IYEOVCRDS	
ETH FRRMEION	
ANLEGAS SASEH	
IERRREPS UBOTYN	
HTE IISHR BPU	
A,IM LEBIE NESIEM NEBLES	

HTE PEPASNR	
ETH MTINIRLAOE	
KORYC ADOR OT BLDUIN	
CW	
NSTA DNA LEIOL	
YDNGI OFR A NDKIR	
PMTUSRTE CYIT	
SNGI RTESTE	
LDO ESRSOC	
OMLLERWC NI ALERNID	
YM ELTF OFTO	
UEHNRG	
EHT XOERB	
HTE RSPEURSE OCREOK	
KISSSE	
RTMOHE NAIDERL	
LIUONCOSL	
HTE LDAY PEYGSG PSAEEC	
OEN LNLIMIO IULDSNBER	

GSSTEU FO ETH NIAOTN	
EHT PYS NI TEH ARI	
JTROAN IEDED	
ON LAÉARB	
ETH UHNRUAGSHA	
BENETWE ETH ANSLCA	
ERAH YM GSNO	
CFLITESENRO	
DDO ANM UOT	
OMBOL	
TEH BTSOREL	
RAUGNDO	
IIHRS DNA PODUR FO TI	
HTE AEDD	
A ELTBRREI BAUYET	
EBNGI PA	
ROF AENRLDSI EASK	
BEMNRVOE OAORTEFNN	
SEEIAVW	
NI EHT ANEM FO TEH ERATFH	

HTE IGESRT AILT	
EGNEDL	
NISDIE MI NDINAGC	
EHT LACNA	
VEAEM	
OT KLLI HTE ICBNETA	
A NHIFTIGG ANM	
BDOYLO UNDSAY	
CGHNISA EESNLPARCUH	
CRONEITURESR AMN	
UALPA	
EMN FO ERLAIDN	
WC,YAON EHT ERRYK RACEND	
FRA OFRM ERISN ELSI	
HWO EW BEWL HTE OMBO	
IYMJMS NNNIWI ECTASMH	
EUSYSLS	
ESWPSASEEKT	
AORHKCSM DAN AKWITSSA	
NYDSAU	

HTE OLNG DOGO AYDFIR	
YSASEC IILLMONS	
HET EAYRL RIDB	
TNHIG TAOB OT UDLIBN	
NGUOY REFOEFND	
TWEYSE RBRETAT	
YM AMEN SI LIYEM	
BOEXD	
AGOMNTS NOEMW	
TEH KLUC FO HTE SRHII	
NFSANII NRABIOW	
SLAIA	
BKCYIOM DAN EM	
WINGTAI ORF IUDNBL	
NA EVLGNIERTSA PCEIE	
EWHN DLINREA AVSDTE	
BEOLN	
IPSNGR MTIGENE	
EENRGLA JNHO NRGEA	
OFOPR	

UJPM	
HTE LISHL FO EIRANDL	
NI AFRE	
LESFI A BEEZRE	
OTHRS LMFSI	
I MA TLFBEAS	
ATOUB AMDA	
A EHNIS FO OIWABRSN	
EOLV NAD ARGE	
A RRBIEETL AUETBY	
TEH LEEGNT GNUNMA	
NIGK FO HTE RALTRLSEVE	
IHWTE YOPN	
ARARG-NEPUOA-H	
IRUSUPT	
HTE DLA OMRF LOD NLRAIDE	
SRAEYDYEST INHDRECL	
GEP O YM TEHRA	
ZEEFRE RFMEA	
HET NEDKA HTRUT	

REMAAPMK	
YNGOU YDSSACI	
ANM FO AARN	
A FMLI IWHT EM NI TI	
ETH SDOWAH FO A UMGNNA	
HTE ISTRUVE	
A LTSEBAF TRSYO	
A IGNNGTIHLAE IFNLLAG	
ACSLH FO HET HSA	
LAL OFR DLO LDRAINE	
BRAGSREB	
EWE LAYD EYTBT	
HTE MNTSICMTOME	
ODENIN	
ODLBO FO EHT ISHRI	
VAEPE KAELNEC	
A WRA FO RDNHECLI	
ETH TSAG	
A OTCRSOD SWRDO	
TEH FRTTOEGNO SIRHI	

URHOG ERDRI	
ESLDIARN STCICKOPEKP	
OWH HRRAY EMABEC A TEER	
TEH EVSWI FO AWSTJOMEN	
TEH ICRVA FO RBAY	
ODGO TOINRAIVSB	
HET MYAOR OFMR LADINER	
DANEK CSAMRSAE	
IFLLNGA OFR A EADCNR	
EOYMNHOON OFR OEN	
EHT YKNA	
DGOL	
ERDA RAHAS	
RATEISECSN	
CHODHEI SNSHACHIEA	
NGAKWI NDE	
ADN ON OEN DULCO VAES EHR	
ETH NFIGGHIT YONNLF	
ILYL FO ARKYNLILE	
HTE RSGEASTNR EMCA	

IKRUEQ	
EHT HIGH CANMODM	
AYPPH EERV ATFRE	
ÁN GLI INNS I DENRADMA	
CEMILAH NLSOLCI	
MNE TA UCLHN	
RUOF ASDY NI ULJY	
KE HAT TERIG	
IRVNAOEC GUREIN	
RNIIODVCG JAKC	
OYRR MOEOR	
QUTEUIN AGVRES	
YAPTEIBIDL	
EAS EVREF	
HTE SOTL IYTC FO Z	
I DTMRAE I OWEK PU	
OYU EMRBMEER ENELL	
HTE EMAZ	
IDHBEN TEH MSAK	
YM HIRSI MYOLL	

ETH ERYA FO EHT RECHNF	
ITUCNRNRSOEI	
GHEYUHA	
YPAPH EEVR RTESFA	
EHT ECRSET FO SLLEK	
NAM CANDIN	
A LVOE IVDDIED	
STSTDUAR	
ONSG OFR A RGYAG OYB	
YARBR NYNDOL	
ZOPETROE	
ETH NTLEEAR	
AEDD MSAN NDCEEIEV	
RCÉ AN ICLEL	
HTE ORTIUDES	
HET HRCUS	
FIFTY EADD NME LGAKNWI	
ECRAIHL	
EHT ITUOBCADN LUCB	
TOPRATI GEAMS	

HSI DNA RSHE	
MZEA	
CIOKM	
ATWH FI	
SMORSOH	
HET TCNUROY RSLGI	
NUJO DAN HET PCKOAYC	
HTE TNIACSKMHO MNA	
EHT CYNGRI GMEA	
ETH HELO NI ETH RONDUG	
EXS NAD YIENLITISSB	
SREYIPTOPR	
GHNTI PEOEPL	
JNONYH AWS	
A NMA FO ON NCAIROMPET	
ERLEB AETHR	
ETMANRLOEW	
HEGSIRACN OFR GERASRH	
URIOSCU NYUJOER	
HET ARDMLEE DNOMAID	

IEMS IÉER	
EHT AMNSDSE MFRO NIIHTW	
TELBRA BNBSO	
HET ECTSRE	
ETH CYLEBERRM OBSY	
WOBCYSO ADN GNLASE	
A TCYI RNDIAGEM	
SYNAR RDTEHUGA	
A IUETQ YAD NI FETBLAS	
,VELO RSIOE	
ELOLBIENR	
LTLIET EITWH LEI	
AWBMGNOO	
HAEDT NO HET CKOR	
SAEJM YOJ:CE 41198-128	
TAEYS TNYUCOR	
FLHDSIGO YMOMER	
TEH RCTSEE FO NROA IINSH	
EHT ANV	
LBTEAT FO ETH BNOE	

HEAFTR DAN NOS	
OSLARBT BYO	
TEH REKYR OGW	
GLEAN	
ORHBMYCERB	
A UTRHREF GTRSEEU	
HET DAGUR	
LBDTAOEH WLEFO TEON	
MGAHO	
ETH DSGLEOR	
EVYELN	
EHT GANEREL	
SP I OEVL UOY	
EHT ENVTSHE MASRTE	
OMCE AKCB OT INRE	
TEH PIPE	
HTE IMRAELC	
NIASAGT ETH WNID	
TOAMNSUIN MORENOU	
ISLOTONIA	

DDEA BSDOEI	
EVLDEBO YMENE	
RAKFN	
PIDANET AYLD	
HET TIPRATO EAMG	
OYJEC NI JNUE	
ROBN DNA RADEER	
AETNDUM	
ETH AAFTISNST	
OLODB RTFUI	
ETH GUHLOP ADN HTE SSART	
TEH NURYGH SSGRA	
TDUSS	
I ESE A AKDR NASRGTER	
NAOR	
HTEENLAP	
RKEOA	
REGNE SI EHT RUOLCO	
ETH CTHRUBE YOB	
OYB STEA IRGL	

EAUGPL ONTW	
DBRDAARCO RNTESGASG	
ETH GNOL YAW OMHE	
XSE NI A CLDO CEMLITA	
TAMLE HEATR	
EERFIAS	
ENUSEICRK WNAL	
CTPRSEE	
LATACINT	
HEOM SI TEH HOER	
SEMO EHSMROT OSN	
HET WADIGNN	
UHEM	
HET IENDSI	
NGIAYP EHT ENRT	
ALRAM	
UAENLRPHEC 2	
CDGANIN TA HAAUSNLG	
AWTH RIHACDR DDI	
IRADNSLE TRATSEGE	

LNKIIGL ONOB	
HET RELUTS ANOCTEVN	
STRTANI DNA IESDOL	
LEOIN FO ETH ENLG	
YHLO OSRSC	
EEATBHN A NDUIBL YKS	
BKOENR LWA	
GNHIT TIARN	
IVFE NUIEMTS FO AHVNEE	
ALPE RYAE	
DLBUIN RSMDEUR	
AINRLSED' ZNASI	
NO HTE EGDE	
HOELW TOLTA ESLO	
HET EIGRRNEFO	
TEEANDIM 31	
NTHGNIO LPESRANO	
IENLN FRMO AIREDLN	
APY HET HOGTS	
EVOL SI HTE RGUD	

Irish Movies 32

ELATHL FREOC	
TTERMSAS NEM	
RE NKANS NCHTI ELNASS	
EWERDSRIVA	
TEH SAEPDPRAIED	
DAAECYNNCS	
EDHIND AEGDAN	
TEH LMEDNAAEG SSERITS	
OHW OEBMBD IMMHABRNGI	
RSM BOSNRW BYOS DVOEMI	
MDRNIAGE HTE IEUQT AMN	
NATYBSD	
OERSI	
AN ÉCADH GIHTF SCLBU	
SANSTI DAN INSENSR	
RIGO ITCY	
IGHH OBOT ENYNB	
HNLICEDR NI SIRCROSFE	
FLLBAUFP	
SETINL CEAGR	
FNAFTI	
MAMLMA	
OWH OT EB PPHYA	
WLSA FO RTICATOATN	
HTE OSTRCA	

SOLUTIONS

Irish Movies 1 (Solution)

AD	Da
3H	H3
HTE TIHMGY ELCT	The Mighty Celt
HTE GID	The Dig
EHT TPIIRS FO TS OILSU	The Spirit of St Louis
RUPE MLEU	Pure Mule
HTE TOLENSG CEDDAE	The Longest Decade
TRAA AROD	Tara Road
AKENT ODWN	Taken Down
AMYFIL	Family
HONGTNI SPLROAEN	Nothing Personal
TLLASE SYDA	Stella Days
EHT DRUCE	The Cured
ERPNLUHECA ISNRGOI	Leprechaun Origins
HET SEOFX FO WORAHR	The Foxes of Harrow
ON NEOTS EUUNRDTN	No Stone Unturned
ANUBLAEREBK	Unbreakable
SLNDIA FO ERTROR	Island of Terror
EHT ATNRMFINO	The Informant
ORGRE TSEMCANE	Roger Casement

Irish Movies 2 (Solution)

NHASD	Hands
EH	He
RTYIHSO FO IMNEAC	History of Cinema
OHCOLS ILFE	School Life
TOLAF KILE A FBTEURLTY	Float Like a Butterfly
HET IACCR	The Craic
NEISSIONRMIT	Intermission
TRREUN OT SNALCUELNAG	Return to Glennascaul
RTHEE ISWE EOWNM	Three Wise Women
STATNEA	Setanta
NSÍOI	Oisín
SYTUD IELRDAN	Study Ireland
ÍOINPT	Poitín
ADM TOBUA BOMAM	Mad About Mambo
EREHT HESWIS ROF MAIEJ	Three Wishes for Jamie
HET ENIDQNETUL AOSSNE	The Delinquent Season
HTE NEHPWE	The Nephew
EHT SBOY FO TS LOSUMBC	The Boys of St Columbs
ECNO	Once
RHTNAOE HORES	Another Shore

Irish Movies 3 (Solution)

HET YMEGOOBAN	The Boogeyman
OHADSW CNRAED	Shadow Dancer
EHT DASHOW FO A NAUNMG	The Shadow of a Gunman
ETH IRCOUER	The Courier
A PRRAEY RFO ETH GDIYN	A Prayer for the Dying
I NTWE NWOD	I Went Down
IITACNT OTNW	Titanic Town
HET UKCL FO EHT IHIRS	The Luck of the Irish
EHT WNDA	The Dawn
CAKBL 74	Black 47
ELEGRNI NI EHT EASYR	Reeling in the Years
ILGR HIWT REEGN EESY	Girl with Green Eyes
NTNAEALTA	Atlantean
EHT LASD	The Lads
KAEERU RTTSEE	Eureka Street
RACTRAH	Arracht
HROTB FO A YOB	Broth of a Boy
LFSOO FO ROEUFNT	Fools of Fortune
EON HNREUDD NNRIGSOM	One Hundred Mornings
NILBD OSIVIN	Blind Vision

Irish Movies 4 (Solution)

TIOTAPRS	Patriots
IGARPMGELI	Pilgrimage
WGGOINR PU GYA	Growing Up Gay
GNKSI	Kings
HTE DGVABASNO	The Vagabonds
LOULTAF	Fallout
EUTONORSIVL	Revolutions
ISIKSGN CAIEDNC	Kissing Candice
FIKCL	Flick
TSIH SI TEH ASE	This Is The Sea
AHAOCETSI	Taoiseach
ESY I CNA	Yes I Can
AND NDA ESBC	Dan and Becs
GNAEELR OJHN NRGAE	General John Regan
RMENDOAO	Marooned
NGHRYU ILLH	Hungry Hill
EHT IIGSNR FO HTE OMNO	The Rising of the Moon
GKINS NI RASSG LATESCS	Kings in Grass Castles
CIHEALM SIDEIN	Michael Inside
RLIECC FO NEISDRF	Circle of Friends

Irish Movies 5 (Solution)

A STACSMIHR RAST	A Christmas Star
ZANOD	Zonad
PKTSACIR ADY	Patricks Day
NO HTE ONES	On the Nose
APSYRLE FO HTE HIAFLTFU	Players of the Faithful
RNYEOO	Rooney
LERTTSCA	Scarlett
A TATSE RPTAA	A State Apart
HET LAWL	The Wall
YM NSHAD ERA CAYL	My Hands Are Clay
TEH HRSII ONNYHEMOO	The Irish Honeymoon
RTA	Rat
HOEM ULRE	Home Rule
EHT YARTET	The Treaty
FNNIDIG JYO	Finding Joy
MHNSAGNA OUHSE	Hangmans House
AWR FO HTE TOUNBTS	War of the Buttons
TGAHUC NI A EREF TATSE	Caught in a Free State
ETH EPIR	The Pier
GAGRAE	Garage

Irish Movies 6 (Solution)

ARLDCE FO GIEUSN	Cradle of Genius
ATINACP LTFHIOOTG	Captain Lightfoot
HET PKECMEAAER	The Peacemaker
HTE ECESRT CTSIUERPR	The Secret Scripture
LEIEL	Ellie
ROMF ETH DRKA	From the Dark
BEUTRLO IWHT EXS	Trouble with Sex
HET RIISH NI AIEAMRC	The Irish in America
EADCN LIXEE CEDAN	Dance Lexie Dance
GNAUEOSDR ILASISON	Dangerous Liaisons
HTE UARQE OLWLEF	The Quare Fellow
OMNLIHEPA	Philomena
HTE OLAHWL	The Hallow
CYR FO HET NIETCONN	Cry of the Innocent
LLIETT LNEIEL LELYK	Little Nellie Kelly
YM HSREORBT RAW	My Brothers War
IWAAEYSDH	Hideaways
SHI OMHTRE	His Mother
NOPE PTOR	Open Port
OMCONAEDN	Moondance

ESEVN GASE	Seven Ages
ERDKPA	Parked
PCANIAST NAD NGKSI	Captains and Kings
NA ANERRG	An Ranger
HET IELPCES	The Eclipse
BLMA	Lamb
EHT HTROALCN RAYSE	The Charlton Years
LYBNMAUL ABYLLLU	Ballymun Lullaby
AFR DNA AYAW	Far and Away
HTSI EOTRH EEDN	This Other Eden
NSUG NI HET RAEHEHT	Guns in the Heather
TEH LSPBAYOY	The Playboys
ASTSET FO RFEA	States of Fear
AYCTUASRN	Sanctuary
MRERDU NI DEEN	Murder in Eden
AITROL	Rialto
NA ONAARSNBTN	An Bronntanas
ILLY FO NERLKIYAL	Lily of Killarney
OCDSI SGIP	Disco Pigs
YSHOUGBOD NI DREILAN	Doughboys in Ireland

ORYBLNOK	Brooklyn
ATRTAATC	Attracta
NEWH EHT KYS ASLFL	When the Sky Falls
ANEN EDVLIN	Anne Devlin
ON ITERSGN ECLPA	No Resting Place
EOSNINAST	Sensation
HET UETQI MNA	The Quiet Man
NI HTE YDAS FO TS TPCKIRA	In the Days of St Patrick
HELTNAEK NEVROUAEMN	Kathleen Mavourneen
HET UCKL FO TEH SIRHI	The Luck of the Irish
EWHN ICRLHAE EMT TTYKI	When Charlie Met Kitty
YM LEFI ROF AENRLID	My Life for Ireland
SWIWOD EKAP	Widows Peak
ERECST OLEPEP	Secret People
ALHO EEFCTF	Halo Effect
OSER FO RALTEE	Rose of Tralee
TREPTY OLPLY	Pretty Polly
ETH RMACH EARH	The March Hare
KKCOWAGNON	Knocknagow
TEH SIIRH NI ICAEMAR	The Irish in America

EHSNENSY	Hennessy
HNELE	Helen
TEH KMAOMRBBE	The Bombmaker
I MARDET I WKEO PU	I Dreamt I Woke Up
HET LMAROOLB FO AMCNEOR	The Ballroom of Romance
ILTGH YARSE WAYA	Light Years Away
LYON MHAUN	Only Human
HET LTAS CONURIN	The Last Unicorn
TEH GRTAE FIENAM	The Great Famine
AKEFIRN SIAGLTRHT	Frankie Starlight
ONFCLIONAESS	Confessional
CLNKUEK	Knuckle
TEH OECLELN NBAW	The Colleen Bawn
GUEAHRDT FO DASNEKRS	Daughter of Darkness
,UOY EM DNA LREAMY	You, Me and Marley
BUIDNL OOODCLHLS	Dublin Oldschool
OWGODTSOH	Ghostwood
VILAE NDA INKICKG	Alive and Kicking
HET NOTNNECI IEL	The Innocent Lie
NI ENNSSHUI RO NI DSAHWO	In Sunshine or in Shadow

Irish Movies 10 (Solution)

A TOSL OSN	A Lost Son
SONMIIS OT PYRE	Mission to Prey
NTIO EHT WTES	Into the West
TEH UQNEE FO ERNIADL	The Queen of Ireland
EFRREE NDA ETH MELDO	Reefer and the Model
ITNRWES DNE	Winters End
I WSA HYPAP EHRE	I Was Happy Here
EHT TAANGREUE	The Guarantee
FERFALEL	Freefall
REFIGON XEGCENHA	Foreign Exchange
ERLIDAN A ATNNOI	Ireland a Nation
EIALLLG NNYEEOIDLMGN	Illegal Moneylending
MENIAF OT EDROMEF	Famine to Freedom
EHT EOCELNL NABW	The Colleen Bawn
ILWD ABTUO RHAYR	Wild About Harry
A HTRGIB DBNAR WNE YDA	A Bright Brand New Day
HET OLNELAIMD	The Medallion
EDRRIS OT HTE SAE	Riders to the Sea
ESE YUO TA ETH APLILR	See You at the Pillar
RCEPAEIEF	Peacefire

Irish Movies 11 (Solution)

HUISMLOST	Soulsmith
ULSRET UNRDETEHA	Ulster Unearthed
IICEVSV	Civvies
EHWSLORWBLIET	Whistleblower
HYIWREA	Haywire
LASNI	Nails
AEDD NLGAO HTE YAW	Dead Along the Way
TFALA TOIVDAENI	Fatal Deviation
A IGLR OFRM HUMAOGSDI	A Girl from Mogadishu
YM RIFNDE JEO	My Friend Joe
TEH RNFOEIMR	The Informer
OLITE DAN EM	Eliot and Me
AKT ADN :IEALF TAERWRDE	Kat and Alfie: Redwater
ETH NOILLE	The ONeill
HET NGAIGHN ELGA	The Hanging Gale
ELID,RAN TEH PSPRSEDEO	Ireland, the Oppressed
OOCKPNU	Puckoon
LDERO TANH ERLINDA	Older Than Ireland
LNPIEA PNACRUELHSE	Leapin Leprechauns
ETH AHYDR UCBSK VEOIM	The Hardy Bucks Movie

MNAOE	Eamon
,HO RM TORRPE	Oh, Mr Porter
RIHSI IEDSNTY	Irish Destiny
LYNO HET DWNI	Only the Wind
HTE SETCR	The Crest
LDWI SEMRCBEED	Wild Decembers
LORL PU YRUO ELSVSEE	Roll Up Your Sleeves
AOMNDR ESSPAAG	Random Passage
CETACELAPB RSIK	Acceptable Risk
SENTHTRG NDA RNOOHU	Strength and Honour
TGILHF FO HET EODSV	Flight of the Doves
KWEA OOWD	Wake Wood
SSNERNI	Sinners
IRAE,HLNGS OG DNWO	Langrishe, Go Down
DAB ADY RFO ETH UTC	Bad Day For The Cut
TEH XOF FO EGARNVOLN	The Fox of Glenarvon
SNAEG BNREWO	Agnes Browne
HTE OBY MORF RCURYEM	The Boy from Mercury
NONAT	Anton
NCTNATENHEM	Enchantment

Irish Movies 13 (Solution)

ORYODHT MLISL	Dorothy Mills
HNEW EADNBNR TEM TRDUY	When Brendan Met Trudy
EGIMSA	Images
QECNLUEAIJ	Jacqueline
ATC FO BELRAYTA	Act of Betrayal
TEH LPUREP XAIT	The Purple Taxi
A TTILEL BTI VT	A Little Bit TV
PESDE GNATID	Speed Dating
PDCTOEIEN	Deception
AAMD NDA UPAL	Adam and Paul
DELNHCRI TA OKWR	Children at Work
EMOR HATN A IIRSCACEF	More Than a Sacrifice
NA RICSSI	An Crisis
AETLTB FO HET BGSIDOE	Battle of the Bogside
SMUASH	Shamus
STOOH OT LLKI	Shoot to Kill
TEH LNTOVIE NYMEE	The Violent Enemy
IHGH TRISSIP	High Spirits
HTE DARO OT EOHERNW	The Road to Nowhere
MBARE	Amber

LSGNICO HTE IRNG	Closing the Ring
NAM BTAUO ODG	Man About Dog
RYRHAS MAGE	Harrys Game
RLAWTTASE	Saltwater
TISACOHCL	Catholics
ERSTCE FO ETH AEVC	Secret of the Cave
STPEE TMEOER	Petes Meteor
HTE OTRNF IENL	The Front Line
RKNBOE OSGN	Broken Song
TEH MRKETAHCAM	The Matchmaker
ECSRAM FO TEH EHBENSA	Scream of the Banshee
FI YLNHC DHA NIVDDAE	If Lynch Had Invaded
CLSINEE	Silence
DRE ORSSE DNA ERPTLO	Red Roses and Petrol
EHSOGTA	Hostage
HTE OYNGU FERSEDONF	The Young Offenders
TEH ERACOL	The Oracle
TEH LEVDSI DRYOOWA	The Devils Doorway
HWO UTBOA OYU	How About You
ATCIPAN TOOTBYC	Captain Boycott

Irish Movies 15 (Solution)

TLOS VSELI	Lost Lives
TEH STLA PTSBEREEM	The Last September
XPEII	Pixie
AFAEBTSKR NO LUOPT	Breakfast on Pluto
IHSIR RFO CKUL	Irish for Luck
OLVSUREES LEAON	Ourselves Alone
SSOEPROFR MTI	Professor Tim
LLGNSAADS	Glassland
TREEBI	Bertie
SIKN NI EHT EAMG	Skin in the Game
IISRH AMJ	Irish Jam
UY GMIN SI NIMA OMD	Yu Ming Is Ainm Dom
CAVRYLA	Calvary
EHT ASLT EUAPLENCRH	The Last Leprechaun
LNPLARE	Parnell
ACL	Cal
NEWH LIA CAEM OT EDLNRIA	When Ali Came to Ireland
HET BAKLC ESEPH	The Black Sheep
LNEDEG FO HTE GBO	Legend of the Bog
ETH ESA	The Sea

Irish Movies 16 (Solution)

TEH KYE	The Key
EAHRAWD ERX	Rawhead Rex
NGSO FO HET ESA	Song of the Sea
EMBRECDE IDBER	December Bride
SSUMCOT	Customs
HDNOSEMA IVDEL	Handsome Devil
EGSARHR	Shergar
RNU ADN UMJP	Run and Jump
NA ENDPENEDTNI OPEPLE	An Independent People
RRAETUSE SLIDNA	Treasure Island
OZO	Zoo
ELARTRACOEC	Accelerator
A AEDT RFO MDA RAMY	A Date for Mad Mary
MIMJSY LLAH	Jimmys Hall
IYEOVCRDS	Discovery
ETH FRRMEION	The Informer
ANLEGAS SASEH	Angelas Ashes
IERRREPS UBOTYN	Perriers Bounty
HTE IISHR BPU	The Irish Pub
A,IM LEBIE NESIEM NEBLES	Mia, Liebe meines Lebens

HTE PEPASNR	The Snapper
ETH MTINIRLAOE	The Eliminator
KORYC ADOR OT BLDUIN	Rocky Road to Dublin
CW	WC
NSTA DNA LEIOL	Stan and Ollie
YDNGI OFR A NDKIR	Dying for a Drink
PMTUSRTE CYIT	Strumpet City
SNGI RTESTE	Sing Street
LDO ESRSOC	Old Scores
OMLLERWC NI ALERNID	Cromwell in Ireland
YM ELTF OFTO	My Left Foot
UEHNRG	Hunger
EHT XOERB	The Boxer
HTE RSPEURSE OCREOK	The Pressure Cooker
KISSSE	Kisses
RTMOHE NAIDERL	Mother Ireland
LIUONCOSL	Collusion
HTE LDAY PEYGSG PSAEEC	The Lady Peggys Escape
OEN LNLIMIO IULDSNBER	One Million Dubliners

Irish Movies 18 (Solution)

GSSTEU FO ETH NIAOTN	Guests of the Nation
EHT PYS NI TEH ARI	The Spy in the IRA
JTROAN IEDED	Trojan Eddie
ON LAÉARB	No Béarla
ETH UHNRUAGSHA	The Shaughraun
BENETWE ETH ANSLCA	Between the Canals
ERAH YM GSNO	Hear My Song
CFLITESENRO	Reflections
DDO ANM UOT	Odd Man Out
OMBOL	Bloom
TEH BTSOREL	The Lobster
RAUGNDO	Durango
IIHRS DNA PODUR FO TI	Irish and Proud of It
HTE AEDD	The Dead
A ELTBRREI BAUYET	A Terrible Beauty
EBNGI PA	Being AP
ROF AENRLDSI EASK	For Irelands Sake
BEMNRVOE OAORTEFNN	November Afternoon
SEEIAVW	Seaview
NI EHT ANEM FO TEH ERATFH	In the Name of the Father

HTE IGESRT AILT	The Tigers Tail
EGNEDL	Legend
NISDIE MI NDINAGC	Inside Im Dancing
EHT LACNA	The Canal
VEAEM	Maeve
OT KLLI HTE ICBNETA	To Kill the Cabinet
A NHIFTIGG ANM	A Fighting Man
BDOYLO UNDSAY	Bloody Sunday
CGHNISA EESNLPARCUH	Chasing Leprechauns
CRONEITURESR AMN	Resurrection Man
UALPA	Paula
EMN FO ERLAIDN	Men of Ireland
WC,YAON EHT ERRYK RACEND	Conway, the Kerry Dancer
FRA OFRM ERISN ELSI	Far From Erins Isle
HWO EW BEWL HTE OMBO	How We Blew the Boom
IYMJMS NNNIWI ECTASMH	Jimmys Winnin Matches
EUSYSLS	Ulysses
ESWPSASEEKT	Sweepstakes
AORHKCSM DAN AKWITSSA	Shamrock and Swastika
NYDSAU	Sunday

Irish Movies 20 (Solution)

HTE OLNG DOGO AYDFIR	The Long Good Friday
YSASEC IILLMONS	Caseys Millions
HET EAYRL RIDB	The Early Bird
TNHIG TAOB OT UDLIBN	Night Boat to Dublin
NGUOY REFOEFND	Young Offender
TWEYSE RBRETAT	Sweety Barrett
YM AMEN SI LIYEM	My Name Is Emily
BOEXD	Boxed
AGOMNTS NOEMW	Amongst Women
TEH KLUC FO HTE SRHII	The Luck of the Irish
NFSANII NRABIOW	Finians Rainbow
SLAIA	Ailsa
BKCYIOM DAN EM	Mickybo and Me
WINGTAI ORF IUDNBL	Waiting for Dublin
NA EVLGNIERTSA PCEIE	An Everlasting Piece
EWHN DLINREA AVSDTE	When Ireland Staved
BEOLN	Noble
IPSNGR MTIGENE	Spring Meeting
EENRGLA JNHO NRGEA	General John Regan
OFOPR	Proof

Irish Movies 21 (Solution)

UJPM	Jump
HTE LISHL FO EIRANDL	The Hills of Ireland
NI AFRE	In Fear
LESFI A BEEZRE	Lifes a Breeze
OTHRS LMFSI	Short Films
I MA TLFBEAS	I Am Belfast
ATOUB AMDA	About Adam
A EHNIS FO OIWABRSN	A Shine of Rainbows
EOLV NAD ARGE	Love and Rage
A RRBIEETL AUETBY	A Terrible Beauty
TEH LEEGNT GNUNMA	The Gentle Gunman
NIGK FO HTE RALTRLSEVE	King of the Travellers
IHWTE YOPN	White Pony
ARARG-NEPUOA-H	Arrah-na-Pogue
IRUSUPT	Pursuit
HTE DLA OMRF LOD NLRAIDE	The Lad from Old Ireland
SRAEYDYEST INHDRECL	Yesterdays Children
GEP O YM TEHRA	Peg o My Heart
ZEEFRE RFMEA	Freeze Frame
HET NEDKA HTRUT	The Naked Truth

Irish Movies 22 (Solution)

REMAAPMK	Mapmaker
YNGOU YDSSACI	Young Cassidy
ANM FO AARN	Man of Aran
A FMLI IWHT EM NI TI	A Film with Me in It
ETH SDOWAH FO A UMGNNA	The Shadow of a Gunman
HTE ISTRUVE	The Virtues
A LTSEBAF TRSYO	A Belfast Story
A IGNNGTIHLAE IFNLLAG	A Nightingale Falling
ACSLH FO HET HSA	Clash of the Ash
LAL OFR DLO LDRAINE	All for Old Ireland
BRAGSREB	Grabbers
EWE LAYD EYTBT	Wee Lady Betty
HTE MNTSICMTOME	The Commitments
ODENIN	Ondine
ODLBO FO EHT ISHRI	Blood of the Irish
VAEPE KAELNEC	Pavee Lackeen
A WRA FO RDNHECLI	A War of Children
ETH TSAG	The Stag
A OTCRSOD SWRDO	A Doctors Sword
TEH FRTTOEGNO SIRHI	The Forgotten Irish

URHOG ERDRI	Rough Rider
ESLDIARN STCICKOPEKP	Irelands Pickpockets
OWH HRRAY EMABEC A TEER	How Harry Became a Tree
TEH EVSWI FO AWSTJOMEN	The Wives of Jamestown
TEH ICRVA FO RBAY	The Vicar of Bray
ODGO TOINRAIVSB	Good Vibrations
HET MYAOR OFMR LADINER	The Mayor From Ireland
DANEK CSAMRSAE	Naked Massacre
IFLLNGA OFR A EADCNR	Falling for a Dancer
EOYMNHOON OFR OEN	Honeymoon for One
EHT YKNA	The Yank
DGOL	Gold
ERDA RAHAS	Dear Sarah
RATEISECSN	Resistance
CHODHEI SNSHACHIEA	Oidhche Sheanchais
NGAKWI NDE	Waking Ned
ADN ON OEN DULCO VAES EHR	And No One Could Save Her
ETH NFIGGHIT YONNLF	The Fighting OFlynn
ILYL FO ARKYNLILE	Lily of Killarney
HTE RSGEASTNR EMCA	The Strangers Came

IKRUEQ	Quirke
EHT HIGH CANMODM	The High Command
AYPPH EERV ATFRE	Happy Ever After
ÁN GLI INNS I DENRADMA	Ná Lig Sinn i nDearmad
CEMILAH NLSOLCI	Michael Collins
MNE TA UCLHN	Men at Lunch
RUOF ASDY NI ULJY	Four Days in July
KE HAT TERIG	Ek Tha Tiger
IRVNAOEC GUREIN	Veronica Guerin
RNIIODVCG JAKC	Divorcing Jack
OYRR MOEOR	Rory OMore
QUTEUIN AGVRES	Unquiet Graves
YAPTEIBIDL	Bipedality
EAS EVREF	Sea Fever
HTE SOTL IYTC FO Z	The Lost City of Z
I DTMRAE I OWEK PU	I Dreamt I Woke Up
OYU EMRBMEER ENELL	You Remember Ellen
HTE EMAZ	The Maze
IDHBEN TEH MSAK	Behind the Mask
YM HIRSI MYOLL	My Irish Molly

ETH ERYA FO EHT RECHNF	The Year of the French
ITUCNRRNSOEI	Insurrection
GHEYUHA	Haughey
YPAPH EEVR RTESFA	Happy Ever Afters
EHT ECRSET FO SLLEK	The Secret of Kells
NAM CANDIN	Man Dancin
A LVOE IVDDIED	A Love Divided
STSTDUAR	Stardust
ONSG OFR A RGYAG OYB	Song for a Raggy Boy
YARBR NYNDOL	Barry Lyndon
ZOPETROE	Zoetrope
ETH NTLEEAR	The Eternal
AEDD MSAN NDCEEIEV	Dead Mans Evidence
RCÉ AN ICLEL	Cré na Cille
HTE ORTIUDES	The Outsider
HET HRCUS	The Crush
FIFTY EADD NME LGAKNWI	Fifty Dead Men Walking
ECRAIHL	Charlie
EHT ITUOBCADN LUCB	The Abduction Club
TOPRATI GEAMS	Patriot Games

HSI DNA RSHE	His and Hers
MZEA	Maze
CIOKM	Micko
ATWH FI	What If
SMORSOH	Shrooms
HET TCNUROY RSLGI	The Country Girls
NUJO DAN HET PCKOAYC	Juno and the Paycock
HTE TNIACSKMHO MNA	The Mackintosh Man
EHT CYNGRI GMEA	The Crying Game
ETH HELO NI ETH RONDUG	The Hole in the Ground
EXS NAD YIENLITISSB	Sex and Sensibility
SREYIPTOPR	Prosperity
GHNTI PEOEPL	Night People
JNONYH AWS	Johnny Was
A NMA FO ON NCAIROMPET	A Man of No Importance
ERLEB AETHR	Rebel Heart
ETMANRLOEW	Watermelon
HEGSIRACN OFR GERASRH	Searching for Shergar
URIOSCU NYUJOER	Curious Journey
HET ARDMLEE DNOMAID	The Emerald Diamond

Irish Movies 27 (Solution)

IEMS IÉER	Mise Éire
EHT AMNSDSE MFRO NIIHTW	The Madness From Within
TELBRA BNBSO	Albert Nobbs
HET ECTSRE	The Secret
ETH CYLEBERRM OBSY	The Brylcreem Boys
WOBCYSO ADN GNLASE	Cowboys and Angels
A TCYI RNDIAGEM	A City Dreaming
SYNAR RDTEHUGA	Ryans Daughter
A IUETQ YAD NI FETBLAS	A Quiet Day in Belfast
,VELO RSIOE	Love, Rosie
ELOLBIENR	Rebellion
LTLIET EITWH LEI	Little White Lie
AWBMGNOO	Bogwoman
HAEDT NO HET CKOR	Death on the Rock
SAEJM YOJ:CE 41198-128	James Joyce: 1882-1941
TAEYS TNYUCOR	Yeats Country
FLHDSIGO YMOMER	Goldfish Memory
TEH RCTSEE FO NROA IINSH	The Secret of Roan Inish
EHT ANV	The Van
LBTEAT FO ETH BNOE	Battle of the Bone

Irish Movies 28 (Solution)

HEAFTR DAN NOS	Father and Son
OSLARBT BYO	Borstal Boy
TEH REKYR OGW	The Kerry Gow
GLEAN	Angel
ORHBMYCERB	Cherrybomb
A UTRHREF GTRSEEU	A Further Gesture
HET DAGUR	The Guard
LBDTAOEH WLEFO TEON	Theobald Wolfe Tone
MGAHO	Omagh
ETH DSGLEOR	The Lodgers
EVYELN	Evelyn
EHT GANEREL	The General
SP I OEVL UOY	PS I Love You
EHT ENVTSHE MASRTE	The Seventh Stream
OMCE AKCB OT INRE	Come Back to Erin
TEH PIPE	The Pipe
HTE IMRAELC	The Miracle
NIASAGT ETH WNID	Against the Wind
TOAMNSUIN MORENOU	Mountains OMourne
ISLOTONIA	Isolation

Irish Movies 29 (Solution)

DDEA BSDOEI	Dead Bodies
EVLDEBO YMENE	Beloved Enemy
RAKFN	Frank
PIDANET AYLD	Painted Lady
HET TIPRATO EAMG	The Patriot Game
OYJEC NI JNUE	Joyce in June
ROBN DNA RADEER	Born and Reared
AETNDUM	Untamed
ETH AAFTISNST	The Fantasist
OLODB RTFUI	Blood Fruit
ETH GUHLOP ADN HTE SSART	The Plough and the Stars
TEH NURYGH SSGRA	The Hungry Grass
TDUSS	Studs
I ESE A AKDR NASRGTER	I See a Dark Stranger
NAOR	Nora
HTEENLAP	Elephant
RKEOA	Korea
REGNE SI EHT RUOLCO	Green is the Colour
ETH CTHRUBE YOB	The Butcher Boy
OYB STEA IRGL	Boy Eats Girl

EAUGPL ONTW	Plague Town
DBRDAARCO RNTESGASG	Cardboard Gangsters
ETH GNOL YAW OMHE	The Long Way Home
XSE NI A CLDO CEMLITA	Sex in a Cold Climate
TAMLE HEATR	Metal Heart
EERFIAS	Faeries
ENUSEICRK WNAL	Cruiskeen Lawn
CTPRSEE	Spectre
LATACINT	Atlantic
HEOM SI TEH HOER	Home Is the Hero
SEMO EHSMROT OSN	Some Mothers Son
HET WADIGNN	The Dawning
UHEM	Hume
HET IENDSI	The Inside
NGIAYP EHT ENRT	Paying the Rent
ALRAM	Alarm
UAENLRPHEC 2	Leprechaun 2
CDGANIN TA HAAUSNLG	Dancing at Lughnasa
AWTH RIHACDR DDI	What Richard Did
IRADNSLE TRATSEGE	Irelands Greatest

LNKIIGL ONOB	Killing Bono
HET RELUTS ANOCTEVN	The Ulster Covenant
STRTANI DNA IESDOL	Tristan and Isolde
LEOIN FO ETH ENLG	ONeil of the Glen
YHLO OSRSC	Holy Cross
EEATBHN A NDUIBL YKS	Beneath a Dublin Sky
BKOENR LWA	Broken Law
GNHIT TIARN	Night Train
IVFE NUIEMTS FO AHVNEE	Five Minutes of Heaven
ALPE RYAE	Leap Year
DLBUIN RSMDEUR	Dublin Murders
AINRLSED' ZNASI	Ireland's Nazis
NO HTE EGDE	On the Edge
HOELW TOLTA ESLO	Whole Lotta Sole
HET EIGRRNEFO	The Foreigner
TEEANDIM 31	Dementia 13
NTHGNIO LPESRANO	Nothing Personal
IENLN FRMO AIREDLN	Linen from Ireland
APY HET HOGTS	Pay the Ghost
EVOL SI HTE RGUD	Love is the Drug

Irish Movies 32 (Solution)

ELATHL FREOC	Lethal Force
TTERMSAS NEM	Mattress Men
RE NKANS NCHTI ELNASS	Er kanns nicht lassen
EWERDSRIVA	Waveriders
TEH SAEPDPRAIED	The Disappeared
DAAECYNNCS	Ascendancy
EDHIND AEGDAN	Hidden Agenda
TEH LMEDNAAEG SSERITS	The Magdalene Sisters
OHW OEBMBD IMMHABRNGI	Who Bombed Birmingham
RSM BOSNRW BYOS DVOEMI	Mrs Browns Boys DMovie
MDRNIAGE HTE IEUQT AMN	Dreaming the Quiet Man
NATYBSD	Standby
OERSI	Rosie
AN ÉCADH GIHTF SCLBU	Na Chéad Fight Clubs
SANSTI DAN INSENSR	Saints and Sinners
RIGO ITCY	Giro City
IGHH OBOT ENYNB	High Boot Benny
HNLICEDR NI SIRCROSFE	Children in Crossfire
FLLBAUFP	Puffball
SETINL CEAGR	Silent Grace
FNAFTI	Taffin
MAMLMA	Mammal
OWH OT EB PPHYA	How to Be Happy
WLSA FO RTICATOATN	Laws of Attraction
HTE OSTRCA	The Actors